At Home

with
Johnny, June
and
Mother Maybelle

SNAPSHOTS FROM MY LIFE WITH THE CASH AND CARTER FAMILIES

BY **Peggy Knight**

At Home with Johnny, June and Mother Maybelle

Snapshots from my life with the Carter and Cash Families

BY Peggy Knight

Copyright © 2004 Peggy Knight Enterprises, LLC

All images copyright © 2004 Peggy Knight Enterprises, LLC, except those on pages 2, 4, 9, 12 (right), 13, 20 (right), 24 (right), 28 (right), 29 (left), 34 (bottom right), 38, 40, 42, 43, 47 (left), 50 (left), 59, 62, 64 (left), 66, 72, and 77.

All text copyright © 2004 Peggy Knight Enterprises, LLC.

Published by PREMIUM PRESS AMERICA

ISBN 1-887654-91-7

Library of Congress Catalog Number 2004105842

PREMIUM PRESS AMERICA gift books are available at special discounts for premiums, sales promotions, fund-raising, or educational use. For details contact the Publisher at P.O. Box 159015, Nashville, TN 37215, or phone toll free (800) 891-7323 or (615) 256-8484, or fax (615) 256-8624.

www.premiumpressamerica.com

Design by Armour&Armour, Nashville, Tennessee

First Edition June 2004

1 2 3 4 5 6 7 8 9 10

To June Baldini

A great friend to the
Carter family and to me

Thank you for helping us
in our times of need

Introduction

BINGO. That's what changed my life forever.

I never dreamed when I went to the Inglewood VFW Club to play bingo one night in 1967 that I'd meet the famous Mother Maybelle Carter. I had listened to her for years on the radio while my sisters made fun of me for loving country music.

The chance meeting with Maybelle—that's what she insisted I call her—led to a wonderful friendship.

When Maybelle's husband Eck got sick, I moved in to help her take care of him. I stayed with Maybelle until she died in her sleep in 1978, the night we played our last bingo game together at the VFW Club.

That's when I started working full-time for June and John. (In public he was Johnny but to me he was always just John.)

All in all, I spent thirty-two years with the Carter and Cash families, doing whatever they needed—cooking, running errands, taking care of them day and night when they were sick. I was with them at their many homes, on tour, and on vacation, traveling to places I never dreamed I'd ever see. Why, I never thought I'd leave the state of Tennessee, much less go to Israel and Europe.

And when I lived with my Mama and eleven brothers and sisters in a tiny house in the Bordeaux section of Nashville, I never dreamed I'd meet so many famous people or become a part of the most famous family in country music.

Over the years I collected a lot of photographs. After June and John died so close together in 2003, the pictures consoled me when I grieved. Through these pictures I revisited the places we'd been and remembered the good times we had.

I'm happy to share this book with the many fans who loved Johnny, June, and Maybelle. I hope you enjoy my memories and pictures.

Peggy Knight
May 2004

At Home

Johnny and June

Dennis Devine is one of John's biggest fans. They first met in February 1960 (above). As long as John was able to perform, Dennis attended as many concerts as he possibly could. Throughout his career, John always made time for his fans. Here he's signing autographs after a show in Omaha in 1965.

The House of Cash in Hendersonville, Tennessee, is home to the Johnny Cash museum, gift shop, and business offices. Sometimes people would get married at the church right next door and come over to the House of Cash for the reception. In this picture from 1974, John is talking to a wedding guest and Brother John Cobalt, pastor of the church.

Long-time fan Barbara Sather from Wisconsin saw June and Johnny perform many times. She took this picture backstage at a concert around 1982, just before the show started.

John sometimes had his stage outfits custom-made, but June bought most of her clothes ready-made. She loved to go shopping in New York and California for dresses like this one. This picture was taken around 1980.

The famous designer Manuel custom-made several stage jackets for John, including this one embroidered with a stylized Great Seal of the United States. He's wearing this outfit backstage before a performance around 1975. You can see more of this jacket in the picture on page 12.

I took this picture
backstage at a concert
around 1990. June had
a lot of fans who loved
her very much, and
here she's showing off a
fruit basket one of her
favorites gave to her.

I took this picture of June in July 1974. She had just finished a concert and was heading back to the motel. I'm not even sure what town we were in—one of the hardest parts of being on tour for everybody is waking up in a different town every morning.

John and his manager Lou Robin get into John's silver Mercedes, parked outside the House of Cash. This was about the only car John ever owned that wasn't black. One day he drove it over to his compound across from his home in Hendersonville, and it got stuck in the mud. He kept trying and trying to drive it out until he burned up the motor.

This was taken on the tour bus, probably around 1980. The bus was nice for traveling: We could cook our own meals, but when we got tired of doing that we'd go to a restaurant. There was always something fun to do on the bus, but we mostly slept in nice motels.

We were ready to go out to dinner around 1984 when June took this picture of John and me. We're standing at the foot of the stairs in the Hendersonville home right in front of the big stone wall in the den.

John's book *Man in Black* came out in 1975.
I took Maybelle up to the House of Cash
for an autographing party. I still have the
book he signed for me then; it's priceless.

In 1986 John wrote
Man in White about
the Apostle Paul. John
did all the research
and the writing. He's
signing a book for a
fan here, probably in
the fall of 1986.

Their fans loved them, and they loved their fans. John and June often hosted events and parties for members of their fan clubs in appreciation for their loyalty and devotion. The fans got to meet them in a personal setting like this fan club breakfast at a Nashville restaurant on June 10, 1982.

June always had a smile and a kind word for her fans. Barbara Sather, a longtime admirer, took this picture in June 1983 at the House of Cash, where June was meeting fans and signing autographs. She's wearing blue, her favorite color because it brought out the blue of her eyes.

June loved to collect and wear furs, so John enjoyed buying her new ones like her fur turban. Here she spreads them out in a limousine in New York. One time she took this picture of me in her bedroom, "the Blue Room," as I rolled around in a bunch of her fur coats and hats. Sometimes June would host fur parties, where she would invite people to her home to buy and sell furs.

I took this picture backstage after a concert, probably in the mid-'90s. June always looked pretty. She knew how to pick clothes so that anything she put on, she looked good in it. She bought this dress on one of her shopping trips to New York.

For several summers in a row, we went to Saskatchewan on fishing trips, complete with chartered planes and Indian guides. When I took this picture, probably in 1980, June was riding on the bus back to Red's Fishing Camp, where we always stayed. That is Red's wife in the background.

John took this picture of June and me in the kitchen
of the house in Jamaica, about 1995. We were heading
out to go shopping in Montego Bay. You can see fresh
fruit in the background—we always had lots of it in
Jamaica, mostly picked from the trees in the yard.

I took this picture of June at her home in Virginia, probably in 1999. You can see a picture of her daughter Rosey on the table behind her, and a picture of Mother Maybelle in profile hanging on the wall. Note the lampshade June made from a linen tablecloth, a favorite hobby of hers.

June always called us her "Ladies in Waiting"—me, my
sisters Shirley and Betty, and Anna Bisceglia, who worked
for her. If anyone had a birthday, June would throw a
party, and nobody got much work done that day. Here,
June is leading the prayer before we eat at Shirley's
birthday party in 2000.

When this picture was taken around 1984, June and John had just done a concert at the Carter Family Fold. Afterward, we all went over to the A.P. Carter Museum for a reception. June's cousin Janette Carter Kelly—A.P. and Sara's daughter—runs the Fold and museum in Hiltons, Virginia.

June and John did a concert in Des Moines, Iowa, in March 1989. Pat Katz, a longtime fan, took this picture of them in the elevator of the Marriott Hotel where we were staying.

June loved flowers. She planted them wherever she lived, and she always had fresh flowers in the house. I took this picture as she checked on the flowers growing at her home in Virginia. This is the old homeplace where she grew up.

John took this picture of me and June in the kitchen of
the house in Hendersonville. I did most of the cooking
when we were at home, wherever "home" happened
to be at the time. Note the fresh roses sitting in the
window sill beside us; you could always count on
having fresh flowers when June was around.

Pictures like this one bring back a lot of good memories. June took this picture at our home in Jamaica in 2001. We were sitting in the dining room, and John and I had been playing dominoes; our score sheet is lying on the table. In the background, you can see the china cabinet with June's dishes, and the curtains June made from tablecloths. She made all the curtains in the Jamaica house from linen tablecloths she bought there.

Over the years, you see some fans so often, they become your friends. Here, John talks with Ronnie Williams from Virginia around 1985. Ronnie came to a lot of the concerts, and he was a big Carter Family fan who especially loved Maybelle and Helen. Barbara Sather from Wisconsin is another fan we saw at concerts many times. She became a good friend, and when she was in town for Fan Fair John invited her out to the house.

Michelle and John Rollins were good friends of June and John in Jamaica, and I took this picture of June on the beach at their house in 1999. The Rollins lived nearby, and we had gone over there to have lunch with them. June always wore a big hat when she was outside in Jamaica, because she was sensitive to the sun.

We did a lot of touring in the mid-1980s, when this picture was taken. John had just come offstage from a performance in Des Moines, Iowa. One of the best parts of being on tour was the chance to meet nice people like superfan Dennis Devine, who took this picture.

At Home

Mother Maybelle and the Carters

I took this picture of June and her sisters Helen and Anita backstage at a concert, probably in the early 1970s. They performed with Maybelle as "Mother Maybelle and the Carter Sisters" and went on tour with Johnny Cash two years before John and June married in 1968. In those days, June and Anita looked quite a bit alike, but you can always pick out June from her big blue eyes—just like Maybelle's.

This picture of Mother Maybelle and the Carter Sisters probably was taken in the early 1950s, about the time they joined the Grand Ole Opry. Maybelle's husband Eck turned down the Opry's offer several times before that because the Opry wouldn't let Chet Atkins accompany them. We had this picture reproduced in 1988 and sold it at shows on the road.

I took this picture in 1976, about two years before Maybelle died. The girls all came to see her at her house on Due West Avenue in Madison, Tennessee, where June lived before she married John. Maybelle moved in when June moved to Hendersonville. The girls took after their mother: always kind and very thoughtful. I never heard them have a cross word with each other, and I never heard any of them raise their voices except to sing.

This picture dates from the early 1970s, taken backstage after a concert when Mother Maybelle and the Carter Sisters were touring with John. After Maybelle's husband died in 1975, I went with Maybelle on tours with June and John, and she would join them on stage for a song or just an introduction. Anita and Helen kept traveling with June and John until Helen passed away in 1998 and Anita had to stop performing because she got sick.

Maybelle always had a great sense of humor. One night she and I were visiting her friend Des Little in New Port Richey, Florida. Des was teasing Maybelle about being dressed like The Man in Black. He said, "What we need to do is make a cowgirl out of you." So he got her a cowboy hat, holster, and gun, then I took her picture. This was about 1975. If you look closely, you can see a picture of June and John on one side of the shelf behind her, and a picture of Maybelle on the other side.

MADISON-BOWL
REBEL HOUSEWIVES
WINTER 73

I met Mother Maybelle Carter playing bingo in 1967, and we hit it off right away. She loved to bowl and had her own team in the league at the Madison Bowling Alley called the Rebel Housewives. Our team—my sister Frances Merriman, Eve Ray, Maybelle, and I—celebrates our win in 1973, one of three times we won the League. I also won the League sportsmanship trophy four years in a row.

Kinfolks often came to visit Maybelle, and we'd all play cards (usually canasta
or rummy) and have dinner with June and John. When this picture was taken in
1973, Maybelle's brother and sister-in-law Toob and Vivian Addington were living
with Maybelle and me, and her sister Merle Fuller and sister-in-law Florida Carter
had come down from Virginia to stay a while. I remember we had all just finished
breakfast and were still in our nightgowns when we had this picture taken.

I helped throw a surprise party for Maybelle on her 65th birthday in 1974. We invited close friends and family to Maybelle's house on Due West Avenue, where June had lived when she was married to Carl Smith. After Maybelle died June donated the property for the Maybelle Carter Retirement Center.

June took this picture of me and Maybelle during the Christmas season of 1973. When Mr. Carter got sick in 1971, June asked me to help Maybelle out with the cooking and taking care of him. June had a great sense of humor: she wrote on the back of this snapshot, "Mama . . . who is that fine looking Chick standing beside you??"

A.P. Carter ran an old grocery store in Hiltons, Virginia, for two decades after he left the original Carter Family in 1943. His daughter Janette Carter Kelly began holding music shows there in 1974. When the crowds outgrew the old store, the Carter Fold was built in 1976 for performances, with a museum for Carter Family items. I took this picture of June and Maybelle helping Janette get the museum spruced up.

This picture of Maybelle and Eck Carter was taken at a banquet around 1968. He didn't play music and he wouldn't go on the road with the family. Until he retired in 1943, he sorted mail on a railroad car.

I snapped this picture of Maybelle as she was waiting to go onstage with June and John. When she got to where she couldn't walk out on stage, she sometimes had a mike set up behind the curtain so she could sing background for the girls. She stopped touring about 1973 or 1974, but we went out with June and John some after Eck died in 1975.

June restored the home place where she was born in Maces Spring, Virginia, and was always working on the house. I took this picture of June's cousin Fern Salyers, June, and her cousin Flo Wolfe.

June and John often did benefit shows at the Carter Fold in Hiltons, Virginia, and for June that was a time to visit family and catch up with old friends. She especially made it a point to visit with shut-ins. On a trip in the early 1990s I went with June and her cousin Fern to visit Maybelle's brother Doc in a nursing home in Hiltons.

Maybelle's brothers, all born in Scott County, Virginia, were known by their nicknames: Duke, Bug, Doc, and Toob. One time Maybelle went to visit Doc in the nursing home and I took this picture of Duke (Dewey L. Addington, born in 1898), Bug (Warren McConell Addington, born in 1918), and Doc (Hugh Jack Addington, born in 1913).

During the visit Duke pulled out his banjo and Maybelle sang to help Doc keep his spirits up. June's Aunt Theta Carter and I took our turn at dancing. Theta was married to Eck Carter's brother Grant.

Maybelle's brother Toob (Milburn) Addington and his wife Vivian lived with Maybelle and me on Due West Avenue for a while. Vivian said, "You do the cooking because I don't like to cook, and I'll do the dishes." Toob took care of the sixteen acres.

Maybelle, June, Helen, Anita, and I went to California about 1975 for the 106th birthday of Aunt Mary Bays, Sara Carter's mother-in-law. Aunt Mary, above, lived to be 110. While we were in California we visited Stella Bays, Sara's sister-in-law. When Sara divorced A.P. Carter, she married his first cousin Coy Bays, and Stella was Coy's sister. I took the picture at the left of Stella and John.

June's daughter Carlene was performing some with June and her sisters Anita and Helen in the mid-1980s, when this picture was taken. The picture appeared on an album that was released in Germany.

At Home
The Family

John and June had millions of fans from around the world, but there is only one Dennis Devine. He was a loyal fan from the 1960s up until June and John died in 2003. He is posing here with Carrie Cash, John's mother, at the House of Cash in 1989.

Carrie Cash was a big, strong woman. When she said something, you knew she meant it. And yet she was also very kind. This picture of us was taken at the House of Cash on her birthday, March 13, 1982.

I loved John and June's families like they were my own. June took the picture above of me with John's brother Roy at the House of Cash where Roy worked security. I remember this picture was taken on the same day that actor Dennis Weaver visited the House of Cash. On the right, John's sister Joanne Yates joins my good friend Skeeter Davis and me at my birthday party in 1980. Joanne and her husband are ministers for the Cowboy Church in Nashville, where a lot of music people go to services on Sunday night.

This picture of John's dad Ray Cash was taken outside the House of Cash around 1980. There was a horseshoe driveway in front of the House of Cash, and every year Ray brought cotton seeds from his farm in Arkansas and planted them inside the horseshoe. After his dad died in 1985, John planted the cotton every year.

Carrie Cash, John's mother, loved to work in the gift shop at the House of Cash, where this picture was taken around 1980. I remember one time she had been to the grocery store and when she got back a crowd of people were standing outside. She was afraid her cold stuff would melt so she just jumped out of the car and ran inside. The only trouble was, she left the car running and forgot about it! The car was still going the next morning.

John enjoys a quiet moment with his grandson Dustin (Kathy's child) in the den of the Hendersonville house, after the excitement of Christmas Day 1993. That's me in the background, cooking in the kitchen.

I took this picture of John's daughter Kathy at the House of Cash, probably around 1988. Kathy grew up in California, then moved to Nashville after she was grown. You can see from the portrait in the background how much she resembles her dad.

June's daughters Carlene and Rosey lived with June and John in Hendersonville, and went to public schools there. Carlene took part in a lot of school activities, like this cheerleading photo from her 1970 junior high yearbook shows, but Rosey never went in for clubs or groups. Carlene was voted Most Popular in her junior high class in 1970. What I remember about her most from those days was that she had a lot of boyfriends. I met some of them, but there was no way I could meet all of them; there were just too many!

Carlene, June's daughter from her marriage to Carl Smith, has been married three times: to Joe Simpkins, father of her daughter Tiffany; to Jack Routh, father of her son John Jackson; and to Nick Lowe. I took this picture of Carlene at Maybelle's house on Due West Avenue in Nashville, right after John Jackson was born. You can see the shadow of John Carter Cash in profile behind Carlene.

Carlene sometimes went with us and performed on tours, like she did for the trip to Paris in May 1989. June took this picture while she, Carlene, and I were out sightseeing.

English rock singer Nick Lowe was married to Carlene. In fact, when he and Carlene got divorced, Nick practically raised Carlene's daughter Tiffany (from her marriage to Joe Simpkins) in England. This picture was taken while John was on tour in England, and I remember Nick performed on stage with John that night.

John liked to work with Jimmy Tittle in addition to welcoming him as a son-in-law. Jimmy and John co-produced the *Classic Cash* album in Nashville in 1987. Here, Jimmy and John's daughter Kathy relax at a party at John's house in Hendersonville around 1990.

Marty Stuart was married to John's daughter Cindy when this picture was taken around 1984. He joined John's band in 1979 and stayed until he left in 1985 to pursue his solo career. Marty remained a friend after he and Cindy divorced in 1988, and I used to tease him that he always showed up at the house just when it was time to eat.

This picture of Rosey was taken at her home in Hendersonville around 1988. It's appropriate that the picture is a little blurry, because Rosey herself lived her life in kind of a blur. She died in October 2003, at the age of 45.

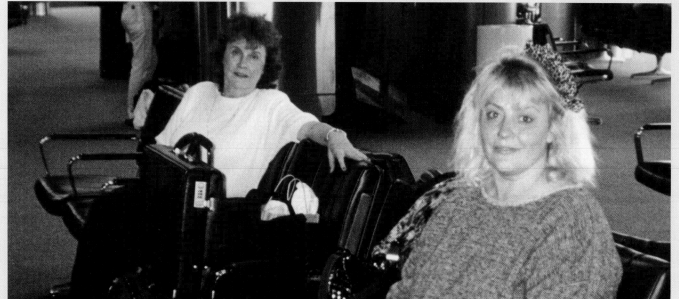

June took both of these pictures of her daughter Rosey. The one above is outside their home in Branson, Missouri, in April 1992. On the left Rosey and I wait at an airport in Germany in 1990, the summer we toured all over Europe. Rosey sometimes performed with John and June in those days—they tried to keep her busy to keep her straight. She had a beautiful voice; I think she sang the best of all Maybelle's grandchildren.

Rosey married Phillip Adams in 2002. I helped her get dressed in a guest room at the house in Jamaica. Later that day I took this picture of Rosey under the decorated arch we created for the ceremony. I went with the Jamaican household staff to the local hardware store to see what we could find. We got wire, metal tubing, and columns, bent it into shape and wired it, then painted everything white. The flowers all came from the yard.

John Carter Cash and I were big buddies back in those days. I used to take him and his friends from school everywhere, like bowling and skating. Here I'm getting ready to take John Carter to dinner after a concert around 1984. John Carter was about thirteen years old when the picture at the right was taken in Saskatchewan where we went on a fishing trip every summer. We had guides who took us out fishing, then when we got back they showed us how to cook the fish on sticks on the open fire. Sometimes we would cook potatoes like that, too. We're wearing matching Bugs Bunny sweatshirts.

At Home
Parties

June loved to give parties, and she knew how to make sure everyone was having a good time. For this party in Jamaica, June made hats for the ladies from flowers in the yard. John took this picture of me, John Murray, June, and Monica from next door. John Murray was in town with his brother Bill Murray, who was filming a movie. We always had plenty of our own fresh flowers for the dining table in Jamaica. June had us set the table with linen tablecloths and napkins, sterling silver, fine china, and crystal for dinner whether we were in Hendersonville, Florida, or Jamaica.

Helen and Anita Carter toured with June and John for several years after Mother Maybelle retired. We celebrated on New Year's Eve with funny hats and noisemakers in Helen's hotel room after a show in Austin, Texas. Anita always liked chocolate ice cream, and I think the vanilla in the foreground is Helen's.

June used to have antique parties and invite friends in to see them and buy them. She displayed the antiques on one dining room table and served an elegant dinner on another table. Here, she's getting ready for one of her antique parties in the 1990s. Barbara Walters, who was in town to interview John and June, bought several plates trimmed in gold.

Margie Wilburn Bowes had a hit with "Understand Your Gal," a response to John's "Understand Your Man" in the late 1960s. She joins him on stage at this party at the Hendersonville house around 1990. After the song, John plants a big kiss on Margie Bowes as Ann Patanan laughs. (John was big on kissing.)

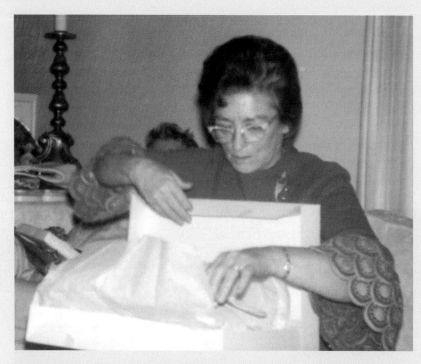

Maybelle's birthday was always an occasion to have a party. Right after I met Maybelle in 1967, June threw a birthday party for her and invited me. I took this picture of Maybelle opening gifts in her living room.

June was out of town for her 65th birthday in 1974, but she sent a lovely pink gown and robe from Rich Schwartz. She got a whole pile of presents that year, including the money tree I made for her. You can see Maybelle's guitar propped behind her chair.

Maybelle and her cousin Sara married the Carter brothers Ezra (Eck) and A.P., and Maybelle, Sara, and A.P. started performing as the Carter Family in 1927. Maybelle played guitar and sang harmony; Sara played autoharp and sang alto lead, and A.P. played fiddle and sang bass. To celebrate their fiftieth anniversary in music, Maybelle and Sara had gold dresses made for the 1977 party at the Carter Fold in Hiltons, Virginia. Afterward, the family went to the home of Gladys Carter Millard, A.P. and Sara's daughter. Gladys presented Maybelle with a cake made in the shape of a guitar.

When June and John had catered parties, they pitched a tent over the tennis courts overlooking Old Hickory Lake. The crowd at this party included singer Mark Collie and his wife Lisa, actress Diane Ladd and her companion, actress Jane Seymour and her husband James Keach.

This picture was taken at a Fan Club breakfast in Nashville in 1982.
Gathered around the table are John's daughter Cindy, his lead guitar player
Bob Wootton, John's granddaughter Jessica, John, June, and Anita Carter.

We were in Jamaica for John's last birthday party on February 26, 2002. He was sick in the hospital for his last birthday in 2003. John was a good sport about wearing a Jamaican hat complete with dreadlocks, and June of course was always willing to try a new hat.

John plays host at his last birthday party, cutting and serving cake to the guests. We didn't have any decorations, so we had to be creative. We found these long fuzzy flowers growing in the yard, and we shaped them on the white tablecloth to spell out, "Happy 70th Birthday Johnny Cash."

When Johnny's great fan Dennis Devine found out that we would be in Des Moines for John's birthday in 1987, he set up a birthday party at the governor's home. Governor Terry Branstad, shown here with Johnny, June, and his wife Chris Branstad, made John an honorary citizen of Iowa.

At Home
Stars

Chet Atkins started playing with the Carter Family before they became members of the Grand Ole Opry. They toured together, and they came to the Opry at the same time. In this picture, Chet is jamming with Helen, Anita, and June during the making of the *Breaking Tradition* album.

It seems like you can hardly get a group of musicians together without them pulling out their instruments and jamming. That's what happened on this afternoon at the House of Cash. John and June's longtime friend Jessi Colter, who came in from Arizona to be with June during her final days, joins John, Helen Carter's son David Jones, and John's guitar player Kerry Marx for an unplanned session.

Grant Turner, the voice of the Grand Ole Opry for nearly half a century, always had time to visit with me the many times that I was there. We would sit and talk in the refreshment area near the Green Room like we did in this photo made about 1972.

John Schnieder came out to the house in Hendersonville while he was in town to record an album. June took this picture of him giving me a big hug in her kitchen. He loved my cooking, especially my country ham breakfasts.

When I was growing up I always listened to the Grand Ole Opry on the radio even though my sisters made fun of me. I liked Little Jimmy Dickens and never dreamed I'd ever meet him—but I ran into him at the Opry about 1980.

A radio program called the Louisiana Hayride went on the air in Shreveport, Louisiana, in 1948 and established itself as the "Cradle of the Stars," a place where country music careers were made. George Jones and Johnny Cash both came to the Hayride in December 1955 and both left late in 1956. Here, George and John share a laugh about Jones' dressing like the Man in Black.

John and June met Prince Charles at a reception during a tour in New Brunswick, Canada, in the mid-1970s. They had a photo similar to this one hanging on the wall in Hendersonville. June wrote on back of my picture: "And what are we all doing in Saint John, New Brunswick?"

John made several
guest appearances on
the television show
"Dr. Quinn, Medicine
Woman" playing the
role of gunslinger Kid
Cole. I went to the
taping on the day this
picture was made on
the set.

June also appeared in several episodes of "Dr. Quinn, Medicine Woman" between 1993 and 1997, playing the role of Sister Ruth. She and Jane Seymour became great friends, and at June's funeral Jane told stories about how she and June would get into giggling fits during the tapings.

June and Jane Seymour take a break from the taping of "Dr. Quinn, Medicine Woman" in 1996 to cuddle with Jane's twins Kristopher and John. They were named for Christopher Reeve, Jane's co-star in *Somewhere in Time*, and John Cash. Baby John, on the right, is a handful; I remember one time he reached up and grabbed big John by the nose.

June took this picture of me and John in his bedroom at the Hendersonville house in 1986. He grew the mustache for his role in the movie *Last Days of Frank and Jesse James.* So far as I know, that's about the only time John ever wore a mustache.

There's never been another performance like it: the last night the Grand Ole Opry performed at the Ryman Auditorium, March 15, 1974. I took Maybelle to the show, and we saw a lot of old friends. I remember Maybelle cried when the curtain came down for the last time.

June met Robert Duvall when she was taking acting lessons from Elia Kazan and they became good friends. The picture at the left was taken one night when he visited her and John in Nashville, and she hired a limousine to take us and some friends to the Opry. I took the picture above on the set of the movie *The Apostle*. June played Robert's mother. In the last scene, June's character was lying in a casket. All of a sudden, just as a joke, June sat straight up! After everybody got through laughing, they re-shot the scene.

John and June became friends with Billy and Ruth Graham in the early 1970s. When they were all in New Port Richey, Florida, Billy and Ruth Graham stayed near John and June in a house built on stilts. Billy and John liked to go deep-sea fishing together. The Grahams attended John's concerts whenever they were in the same area, and John sang at the Billy Graham Crusades. They often visited the Grahams at their home in North Carolina.

Ruth Graham was a great help to me in the kitchen. She always made the coffee when they were visiting us. One time they went deep-sea fishing and caught a lot of shrimp, and Ruth helped Maybelle and me cook them for dinner. June and John used to host Christmas parties at the Hendersonville house, until they became frail and started going to Jamaica every year right after Thanksgiving. This picture of me and Ruth was taken at one of the last Christmas parties in Hendersonville.

Before John married June, he lived in an apartment with Waylon Jennings on Russell Street in Madison. John told me the place was filthy because neither one was very good at housekeeping. June took this picture of John, me, and Waylon at a party at the Hendersonville house about 1980.

John's big fan Dennis Devine took this picture in Omaha, Nebraska, in 1967, shortly before June and John were married. What a cast of talent! In the front are John's manager Saul Holiff, June and John, Marshall Grant, and W.S. Holland. In the back are Carl Perkins, Don Reid (Statler Brothers), Helen Carter, Phil Balsley (Statler Brothers), Luther Perkins, Harold Reid (Statler Brothers), Lew DeWitt, Maybelle, and Anita Carter.

One time when June and I went to
the Opry, we saw Michael Douglas.
I had met his father in Washington
when both John and Kirk Douglas
received the 2001 National Medal
of Arts award from President
George W. Bush. John starred with
Kirk Douglas in one of the last
great westerns, *A Gunfight*.

Dennis Weaver, who starred on television in "Gunsmoke" and "McCloud," dropped by the House of Cash while he was in Nashville on business. I was working in the gift shop and museum at the time, so I called June and John and they came over. Visitors had an unexpected surprise as all three stars signed autographs.

John performed at a private party for International Society of Poets in Washington D.C. That's where I met Florence Henderson, who was also there signing a book. I met actor Charlton Heston there, too.

Shared Memories are the Best!

International Society of Poets

Florence Henderson

Larry Gatlin was always
a big admirer of John.
He did shows with John
from time to time, and
he often came to his
concerts.

One night I went to the Opry and bumped into Tony Joe White, who recorded "Polk Salad Annie." He was a good friend of Anita Carter's but I had never met him until that night. Anita just loved his music.

Whenever friends from Florida were in Nashville, we usually took them backstage at the Opry. Lisa Ovenrader, her husband, and their parents were in town and I took them to the Opry where they got to meet Roy Acuff. They were very excited. Lisa is a former Miss Teenage America.

Two of June's good friends were in town on the same night in 1980: actor
Robert Duvall and her longtime best friend Rosemary Edelman. A bunch
of us had our picture made together backstage at the Opry: me, former
Pittsburgh Steeler Lawrence Elkins, Rosemary's sister Katie Edelman,
Anita Carter, Duvall, June, and Rosemary. Rosemary Edelman loved my
cornbread and biscuits. Many times I'd make a big batch of cornbread
and overnight it to Rosemary in Los Angeles.

Lots of people that I cooked for over the years had favorites that I made. The morning this picture was taken in 1998, the Statler Brothers had come to visit John at the Hendersonville house. I made a light breakfast with sausage rolls, one of the Statlers' favorites. June took this picture of Don Reid, Phil Balsley, me, Jimmy Fortune, and Harold Reid. On the mantle behind us are brass sculptures of June, John Carter, and John.

Willie Nelson and John go way back. They did concerts and recorded albums together. The picture at the right was taken backstage at a concert June and John did with Willie. The shot of Willie Nelson, me, and David Stringfield was taken backstage at a show. David was the head of Baptist Hospital in Nashville at the time. In December 1988, when John was at Baptist for open heart surgery, a friend and his fiancée came to visit. He knew John was an ordained minister, and he wanted John to marry them. John said it had to be right then. June said she'd stand up with them. David happened to be visiting, and John asked him to be best man. I went downstairs and bought flowers for the bride's bouquet. John married them right on the spot.

Kris Kristofferson and John go back to the days when Kris was sweeping floors in a Nashville studio and passing songs he'd written to John. They recorded together as the Highwaymen: Willie, Waylon, Kris, and John. This picture taken backstage at a concert shows Kris's wife Lisa, John holding Kris's son, June, and me.

Kix Brooks came to a party at June and John's home in Hendersonville. I had met his partner Ronnie Dunn and heard him sing "Boot Scootin' Boogie" for the first time when I was staying with Anita Carter.

June loved to sit outside in Jamaica and play her autoharp. Now that she's gone, I wish I could still hear those sweet chords. I took this shot of her sitting on the porch around 1999.